punching the teeth from the sky

brenton booth

epic rites press

First edition. Printed in the USA.

Edited by Wolfgang Carstens

Poetry by Brenton Booth
brentonbooth.weebly.com

Exterior by R L Raymond
www.rlraymond.ca

ISBN: 978-1-926860-54-1

Epic Rites Press publications are distributed worldwide by Tree Killer Ink. For more information about *Punching The Teeth From The Sky* (and other books and publications from Epic Rites Press) please visit the Epic Rites website at www.epicrites.org, or address Tree Killer Ink / Epic Rites Press: 33 Sioux Road, PO Box 80002 Woodbridge, Sherwood Park, Alberta, Canada T8A 5T4.

Epic Rites: any press is only as "small" as its thinking.

ACKNOWLEDGEMENTS

The author would like to thank the editors of Chiron Review, Mas Tequila Review, Dead Snakes, Zygote in my Coffee, Your One Phone Call, Zombie Logic Review, Poetic Pinup Revue, Paper & Ink, Poems For All, Horror Sleaze Trash, and Bold Monkey for originally printing some of these poems.
And Wolfgang Carstens for being one tough beautiful motherfucker!

Contents

punching the teeth from the sky

brenton booth

epic rites press

UNTITLED

The saddest thing
about death
is
most of us
don't lose
much.

PALE BLUE EYES

We used to get drunk
and dance slowly in
our tiny lounge room
thin and gaunt with
little money and bad
jobs
though happy to not
be a part of things
not to be trapped in
the false wheel of
success that never
goes anywhere
her with an empty
canvas
and me with an empty
page
hungry and wounded
but in love
individuals together in
a world of faceless crowds
dancing in our small
apartment
not needing another
thing
and I wonder if she
would remember now
the magic of all those
afternoons, mornings
and nights in her large
house with full cheeks
and bank account and

the kind of partner she
swore she'd never need
again
my guess is like me she
does her best to forget
those special memories
that do nothing now but
sting
and remind us of all that
got lost along the way.

RIPPED OFF

His face was bright red
and clothes stunk of
piss, shit and years of
addiction and he stood
next to the hot dog stand
at Woolloomooloo begging
for money "It's not for
drugs!" he exclaimed
like a poor desperate
animal. Everybody walked
around him, some snarled
and others chuckled at him.
No one was willing to give
him a cent. I took out my
wallet and got out everything
inside it and handed it to him.
Everybody gave me dirty looks.
But I knew the junkie's name
was Bruce. We used to do drugs
together many years ago. The
money I gave him wasn't really
for him. It was for the Gods.
For sparing me.

IN THE CAGE

It started pouring down thick
sheets of water and it was
8:09pm on Boxing Day 2010
and both my feet had calluses
and I'd just finished a 50 hour
week and would begin another
one tomorrow and I looked at
my Christmas present
it was a Randy Couture figure
I then thought of when I went
to Las Vegas and trained at his
gym
sparring in his cage and doing
reasonably well —
though we all have our victories,
most smaller than we'd like
though big enough to allow
us to keep them out of the reach
of others
and tonight like everyone else
I know another year will be gone
in a week
and I hold on to whatever I can
to keep me going.

SPACE

I was in my room
when John from
across the street
came in.
We were good friends,
he was a year younger
than me.
In the kitchen my
mother was cooking
and my father was
drunk on the
front porch
drinking—more
and more.
I had my Lego
blocks out.
John looked worried,
he asked me if he
thought we could
build a spaceship
and fly away to
another planet:
I wasn't sure
but I thought the
idea was good—
I wanted to try it.
When I said, 'Yes.'
The worry left his face.
I then told him he'd
have to go home
and get his blocks

too — the more blocks
the better our craft
will be, I said.
He looked worried
again.
Suddenly all the dogs
living in our
street started
barking;
that could only mean
one of two things:
either the mailman
was in the street
or
John's father was
stumbling home
drunk from
the pub:
we both knew the answer.
'Don't worry about them.
we can build a great ship
with just mine.'
'Yea.'
'Yea.'
We began sorting
through the blocks
and carefully
joining them.
We were going
to space
and we could
already feel
it.

We were both laughing
and our plan was
to just fly
around up
there,
just the two of us:
and we'd only
land when we
needed food —
it would only be us
and the open skies.
My mother pushed
open my door.
'What's that stupid
thing?' she said.
Neither of us
answered.
John went home
and I went to
the kitchen for
dinner. My
father was there already —
drunk and angry.
As I sat there I
thought about
the spaceship.

LOST

Back in the suburb
I escaped from eighteen
years ago
sitting at a table with
the toughest guys at
the bar
talking about fighting
and fucking
ready to beat the crap
out of anyone who looked
at us the wrong way
or screw any woman that
showed any interest
the whole table with nothing
and no chance for a better
future
except me
I had the poem and a job on
the boats in the city
my only problem was coming
back to this place
where time stands still
forever.

SUNDAY AFTERNOON MAGIC

Sunday afternoon listening
to a guitarist play Bach and
hoping for words
it doesn't matter if they aren't
as good as the music I am
listening to —
they rarely are:
but the desire is always
there,
the music is loud —
really loud
to block out the sound of
my neighbours
who sit outside with their
young children and their
endless talk talk talk
not listening to music
not understanding music
seeing only themselves
and their completely
banal existences as music
and truly important;
and on this Sunday afternoon
I thank the Gods for people
like Bach and Rabelais and
Shakespeare and Plato and
Saroyan and everyone else
that chose something more
than the ordinary
something more than their
own personal comfort

to bring magic to a world
dominated by bland, conservative,
forgettable people
and keep hope alive for all the
rest of us.

THE UP AND DOWN

All things change
the moments that
cut through stone
like melted cream
the faces you wish
would always want
you near
the easy times when
you assume your
own perfection
it's the way of
things:
good
bad
certain
uncertain,
days without problem
nights you pray will
never end
or
minutes harder than
death
and nights you'd prefer
to forget
it is the truth of life
the thing we all know
and must accept,
laying in bed now
on this Monday night
in Sydney
writing these words

in a notepad and thinking
about the absolute magic
of her —
wondering if we will ever
lay together in this bed
again.

CRESCENDO

Tchaikovsky's *Suit Number 3*
on a winters evening
in my small art deco apartment
in Potts Point
painting the crème walls blue,
taking away the monotonous sounds
of my neighbours,
opening the windows,
opening the blinds,
opening all the doors in my home;
dancing like a finely tutored soloist
along the empty shelves, cupboards,
drawers, picture frames;
moving with such grace and brilliance
that even the walls now start to disappear;
there are no longer any walls
and the ceiling and roof have turned
into raging flames
that shine like the reflections of truly ornate
jewellery made by the hands of
the finest craftsmen,
and it's no longer Wednesday, or Thursday,
or Saturday, Sunday, Monday, Tuesday, Friday —
the day doesn't mean a thing anymore
the bank statement doesn't mean a thing anymore
neither does the job,
the ex-partner,
the career;
nothing means a thing as the crescendo
arrives and through the smoke thousands
of baby stars fill the infinite sky

and they shine like spotlights onto the soul,
cleansing and restoring it to the way it was
before life,
before time,
before the great burden of living took hold;
and I am alone now on a foreign island
with waves gently massaging the shores
and supernovas lighting up the skies;
there is no electricity,
or money,
or automobiles,
or people,
or work,
or expectations,
or prejudice;
just a full palette of magnified rainbows
painting even the most distant stars,
and a complete and unabridged
sense of total fulfilment—
and I stay there on that island
for an eternity,
a lifetime,
a million years;
then slowly I can see the crème walls again;
I can see the drawers, cupboards, and shelves
again;
I can see the sofa, refrigerator, toaster, toilet,
bed, wardrobe, sink, servery, table, bookcase,
doors, ornaments, floorboards, pictures, books,
laundry basket, fan, towels, toilet paper, food,
speakers, and records again;
and Tchaikovsky has finished playing.

SUICIDE SCARS

Look at those marks on that girl's
arms. I counted seven. She has tried
to kill herself seven times and she is
still just a teenager. There are people
out there with bad health that would
give anything to have her life. I have
no respect for her. She is a complete
waste of life. A total loser! he said. Do
you think I am a loser? I said. Of course
not. Well when I was her age the only
difference between me and her was
courage. I never could get the strength
to break through my skin and veins, just
sat for hours on more than seven occasions
with a sharp knife pressed tight against
my forearm. Knowing it was the only
way, I said. He went silent. What could he
say. He was one of the lucky ones, that
didn't understand how bad things could
actually get.

PRELUDE

When I was ten I used to ride
a skateboard all the time. I'd
often ride alone outside an
abandoned house on a dead
end street I had found. It was
great: there was no one to
complain about the noise. I
was ambitious then. I had seen
these guys riding skateboards
on television, and wanted to
ride like them. And at that age
I knew I could, I could do
anything I wanted. I would
practice for hours. Knowing it
would eventually make me
rich and famous and I'd never
have to work a crappy job like
all the adults I knew. One day
I tried a trick and landed on my
face. Blood poured out of my
mouth and nose. I started
skating home. On the way a car
pulled up next to me. It was a
neighbour driving home after
a long shift on the register at
the local supermarket. "My god,
look at you. What have you done
to yourself?" she said. I didn't
answer. And wondered if she
ever asked herself the same
question.

REASON

The days join
as one into
one long
struggle
music helps
but doesn't
last,
the animals
got it
right;
they never
tried to
be more —
and never
failed
like us:
with
religion,
money,
murder,
suicide,
countries,
politics,
depression,
depravity,
disease:
enough disease
to destroy
a thousand
worlds;
though there

are those
moments,
those seconds,
those times,
where the
true reason
for all this
insanity comes
clear —
like right
now:
laying naked
with her
in the
bathtub
on a Thursday
afternoon
the water
gone cold
but neither
of us wanting
to get out
and lose
this moment
forever.

WHAT'S LEFT BEHIND

He stopped drinking and
smoking and cut out meat
and milk from his diet and
started reading books on
meditation and would
meditate for over an hour
every night
he went from having one
of the shortest fuses I knew
of
to being the most understa-
nding man I had ever met,
it was amazing:
I'd never seen a transforma-
tion like it:
two years later he died of
cancer at only thirty-three
leaving behind a wife, child
and two wasted years.

CARAVAN

When I was sixteen I spent the summer
holidays with my father. We watched old
movies and drank Jim Beam outside his
caravan while Mozart drifted from the
speakers inside. He never let me drink
much—I was always satisfied with one
or two anyway—my guess is he saw
himself in me, and the problems
excessive drinking had created in his life.
Living out his final years in a caravan in
a suburb he hated, but had no choice
because of past mistakes—mostly due
to the bottle. Though both of us smiling
and content. Me still a child, and him
happy with the undeserved company.
With every day feeling like victory. In
a perfect summer, that unfortunately
couldn't last for either of us.

BOTH AFRAID

That night we sat on a seat
in Hyde Park. I drank from
a slurpee we bought earlier
from a 7-Eleven on Oxford
Street. We held hands and
looked at the statue of Captain
Cook. He told me the night was
perfect, though he was afraid
to hold my hand in public. I
told him not to worry. It's fine
for you, you're big and can fight.
I'm small and weak, he said.

A few weeks later in his bedroom
I cried tears of complete guilt and
couldn't do it.

Things were never the same between
us after that.

CEMETARY

When we first got cars we
would meet of a night and
drive for hours in the
darkness. Most of the time
we'd end up stopping at
graveyards. They really
interested us then. We'd
sit on someone's grave
drinking whiskey and
talking. We were never
afraid of ghosts — we
knew they were just
invented to make
otherwise dull places
seem more exciting.
Sitting in those graveyards
of a night seemed to calm
us. There was nothing
unknown there — just death.
Everything was simple there,
in a time of great confusion for
us all. After a while we stopped
meeting up. We all changed and
went our separate ways — rarely
even seeing each other anymore.
All working full-time jobs to pay
our way in society. In buildings
that no matter how hard I tried to
find another comparison, felt exactly
like those graveyards.

SEARCHING FOR HEMINGWAY

The taxi arrived at the
hotel in Havana at 8pm
it was raining though he
still recognized it from
all the pictures he had
seen over the years
he paid the fare and
stepped out of the taxi
3 porters ran for his
luggage
he was already carrying
it but the strongest of
the bunch eventually
wrestled it free
he wasn't sure what would
happen
at the front desk he asked
if Hemingway's room was
available
100 dollars, said the clerk
with a big smile
(he later learned that was
more than 3 times what it
was worth)
the room was quite big for
a hotel room
with a small balcony with
a view of mostly rooftops
the porters wouldn't leave
he gave them each a dollar
note

Eat! eat! they said
No, no, drink! Get me drink!
he said
they quickly scattered like
insane rats
he looked around the room
he thought about his trip
from Sydney to here:
would it be worth it?
the porters all ran in at the
same time
each one with the same bottle
of rum
he made them sweat a bit
then took all 3
he paid each of them then told
them to leave
he locked the door behind them
took off his shirt and shoes
and stood on the balcony with
an open bottle in his hand
had his first hit
and waited.

THE WOUNDS WE WON'T LET GO

Our biggest mistake
is reliving wrong
over and over,
until we can
no longer even
remember the pain it caused,
only the criminal intention
behind it—
and it fills us up completely
with a rage
like the initial pain did before
it went away,
though through our refusal
to forget won't go away;
first destroying us:
quite often more.

FANTE IS WITH ME TONIGHT

In a small room in Bunker Hill
I clip my toenails then open
the blinds
I can see a building
lots of windows
I stick my head out the
window and turn it
and see the Wells Fargo
Car Park (I know this
because the name is
looking at me)
I then close the blinds
and turn on the tap
I wait a few minutes
then fill a plastic cup
I drink the water quickly
and afterwards screw
up my face
I hope that water doesn't
make me sick, I then
thought. Sitting alone
in a cheap room. An
unpublished writer
with a full notepad
and the belief that I
will one day be great.
On the edge of the soft
bed. Listening to the loud
fan, and not hearing another
thing.

THE BUSTY BLONDE

She left me at 5am
to go back to her
husband and kids.
I met her at midnight
at the local bar. I was
strutting around like
the toughest guy on
earth. "If you're so
tough, show me your
hard-on!" she said.
I sat with her. She
had coke and shared
it with me. A few hours
later we were naked.
She sucked me but I
couldn't get it up
because of the coke.
"Not much use, are
you." I told her to
lay down and open
her legs and went to
work. She moaned like
a virgin. "Just imagine
what I could do if I had
a boner." Well I jiggled
it and shook it and she
tried sucking me a few
more times but it just
wouldn't work. And now
all I can think about is
that beautiful pussy—

with a hard on and
nothing to do with it.

RE-READING CHEKHOV'S THE SEAGULL

Tonight you are here
with me once again
with open heart,
and mind,
giant feelings,
and wisdom beyond barrier;
I can remember 15
years ago
when we first met
at the time I was
near the end
though your writing
showed me both
truth and possibility —
two things I'd never
seen anywhere before —
and I immediately shelved
the suicide plan
instead quitting my tiresome
job
and living on only boiled rice
and water
so I could not work for as long
as possible
and hopefully learn to write
like you;
and I spent thousands of
inspired hours writing and
learning that I could never
write like you:
only like me —

and that's why writing is so
great,
and still to this day
keeps me going;
though when you're around
that is never a concern for me:
you saved my life back then,
or maybe just started it;
my greatest teacher:
who deserved so much more.

TOGETHER

Naked at 5pm on
a Friday
on her silk sheets
my left arm under her head
and right arm on her stomach
our body's linked
and me feeling her soft
slightly nervous breaths
and her feeling mine —
naked and silent
the world at war outside
but we are protected
unconscious to it now
our pulses together
our heads on the same pillow
though deep inside a slight fear
the fear that this
could come
to an end.

WOUNDED BY THE DAY

Sometimes
the blade
is so sharp
the hands
can barely
push it away
and even if
they do
you still end
up bleeding.

THE END

If we just accepted
that there is nothing
for us out there
that the gardens will
always be fenced
that the loves will
always be costly
that the dreams will
always be nightmares
that the jobs will always
be unwanted
if we just accepted
that that our heroes
will mostly fail us
that the mirror will
never show us
that the food will
never fill us
if we just accepted
that our lives were
meant for nothing
that our pains were
meant for nothing
that our joys were
meant for nothing
if we just accepted
that over there is
the place we always
dream of
and right here the
place we secretly

yearn to escape
if we just accepted
that the poem
means nothing
that truth means
nothing
that the individual
means nothing
if we just accepted
that we are completely
powerless and mean
nothing
we would finally be
just like them
who willingly accepted
this death
long ago.

PUNCHING THE TEETH FROM THE SKY

Quit my job
bought a computer
hired a car
drove to Canberra
went to the national gallery
found Pollock's *Blue Poles*
sat looking at it
for 30 minutes
went to the toilet
looked at it again for
another 20 minutes
left the gallery
got in rental car
cried thinking of it—
can't explain why?
drove to Jindabyne
got a room
tried to sleep
following day at Charlotte
Pass standing on top of the
Summit
was so cold I
decided to head
to the
sun
15 hours later I'm
in Byron Bay
get a bottle
and a room
head out at 8pm
to see what

the bars are
like
meet Darren
one of the locals
he says I've got on
a gay shirt
but that's ok
you're alright Robert
you're alright
tells me he's
a pussy
yea, I say
yea, been losing lots
of fights lately
really — how many?
two in the last
6 months
how often do you fight?
just about every
night
had 6 rounds
of doubles and Darren's
friend doesn't like
me
thinks I'm a fag
no a cop
no even worse — both
Darren shakes my
hand and says
goodbye
I stumble to
another bar
drink

get back to room at 4am
can't sleep
drank enough to
keep me over the
legal driving
limit for about
24 hours
decide to do
something touristy
get the shuttle
to Nimbin at 10am
meet a pot addicted
Canadian on the bus
he's reading *Fear and
Loathing in Las Vegas*
we talk writers
when we got to
Nimbin ate
a bunch of hash
cookies and
smoked a couple
of joints
with the Canadian
lost all sense
could barely move
a minute seemed
like an hour
somehow bought
a pizza and got
back to my room that night
pot didn't wear
off for another
6 hours

next day I
called by my mother's
place
had dinner
then headed
to Coffs Harbour
from her home in Lowanna
got there and
went to a bar
got a drink
some good girls
would watch the football
first on the pubs
TV screen
then look for company
Cowboys flogged
Tigers
was happy
bought another drink
headed
to a blonde and
brunette
spoke
they turned their
heads the other way
spoke some more
silence
moved to the exit
got a local newspaper
found the
whorehouse
Monique didn't look
so good but

I paid and fucked
her anyway
it was over in a few
minutes
didn't even give
me a blowjob first
or kiss me on
the way out
Coffs Harbour whores
are not Sydney
whores that's
for sure
drove back
to my mother's place
an hours drive
up a steep unlit
mountain
somehow made
it around all
those bends at 1am
without killing
a single animal
or myself
opened the front
door
my mother told
me to turn off
the front light and
lock the front door
from her bedroom
suddenly felt bad
for being such
a horrible

son
slept easily
dreamt I had
special powers
could see through
any lies and shoot lasers
from my fingers
was the number 1 tool of
the government
woke up and shivered
Lowanna is no
Kings Cross
It's cold cold cold
wanted to get away
from the cows,
horses, sheep, houses,
backyards, dirt streets
and grass as soon
as I could
drove back to Sydney
checked the car
had a couple
of big scratches
I couldn't remember
doing
would now be up for the $200
excess
dropped off the car
headed back to my
apartment
was a mess
and had the damp smell
of a cave

my home
sat on my old sofa
and thought about
all the money I spent
felt bad
knowing I had
no work and
was broke
didn't know what
to do
that's when I got
out the computer
I bought
and wrote this.

ABOUT BRENTON BOOTH

Brenton Booth (b.1978) lives in Sydney, Australia. He has worked as a wildlife park attendant, dishwasher, bartender, security guard, cashier, actor, blackjack dealer, cleaner, usher, tour guide, clothing salesperson, and is currently a deck hand. He started writing when he was nineteen and had his first poem published when he was thirty-three. He has been published widely over the past few years. The poems in this collection were written between 2004-2016. He can be reached at brentondeanbooth@gmail.com. To read more of his work visit brentonbooth.weebly.com

www.ingramcontent.com/pod-product-compliance
Lightning Source LLC
Chambersburg PA
CBHW071740020426
42331CB00008B/2102